I0412208

WHAT TO EXPECT WHEN
YOU'RE SELF-PUBLISHING

A VISUAL GUIDE FOR BEGINNERS

SYLVIA CARY

TIMBERLAKE PRESS . LOS ANGELES

ISBN 979-887296-335-6

First Edition. Printed in the United States.
Subject: Reference / self-publishing—United States

SPECIAL ACKNOWLEDGMENT - DAN POYNTER

To the late Dan Poynter, the man who helped invent today's self-publishing Industry and make it into a "thing."

DAN POYNTER, seen here as the main speaker at a Los Angeles writers' event.   Photo: Sylvia Cary

"We have what we seek. It is there all the time, and if we give it time it will make itself known to us."

– Thomas Merton, prolific author, poet, monk, scholar, mystic, theologian, social activist, speaker, and scholar

Cover Graphic of Gutenberg's Printing Press – Pixabay.com

The Literary Ducks   Photo: Sylvia Cary

DEDICATION

For my daughters, Jessica and Claudia; my grandchildren, Lily and Lyle, and in loving memory of my husband, Lance Henrik Wolstrup, and my sister, Eve Cary.

CONTENTS

INTRODUCTION

*P*hoto: Visualhunt

Does self-publishing seem like it's just too hard?

ARE YOU A SELF-PUBLISHING DROPOUT?

"OMG! I'm totally overwhelmed. I had no idea self-publishing a book had so many MOVING PARTS! Help!" — freaked-out newbie self-publisher

THE SELF-PUBLISHING ADVENTURE

Thousands of books are published daily, including many by self-publishers, perhaps like you, eager to see their work in print. The trick is not to drop out before it happens just because you hit a snag.

Often writers begin their self-publishing journey enthusiastically but find their momentum wanes due to fear, perceived complexity, or intimidation by the technical aspects. However, giving up is unnecessary. Self-publishing, particularly on Kindle Direct Publishing (KDP), is accessible and FREE. This step-by-step guide aims to simplify the process for first-timers, making

subsequent attempts smoother. It's particularly helpful for visual learners, with images illustrating key steps and website stopovers along the way.

SO WHAT IS SELF-PUBLISHING EXACTLY?

Self-publishing, or "Print-on-Demand" (POD), utilizes digital files to print books individually, unlike the traditional bulk printing methods. Also known as independent or "indie" publishing, the Internet has democratized the publishing process, enabling writers to independently handle the writing, design, formatting, printing, distribution, and marketing of their books from anywhere.

10 PERKS OF GETTING PUBLISHED?

1. Establishes expertise
2. Benefits your business
3. Acts as a marketing tool
4. Generates income
5. Offers service to others
6. Contributes to giving back
7. Leaves a legacy
8. Fulfills creative desires
9. Promotes personal growth
10. Acts as a stepping stone to new opportunities

IS SELF-PUBLISHING LIKE VANITY PRESS?

Historically, way back before the Internet and digital technology, the only alternative to traditional publishing was costly vanity presses, requiring authors to pay for the typesetting and printing of their books. Now, digital platforms have transformed the landscape, making self-publishing accessible and affordable for everyone.

"Wear the old coat and buy the new book."
– Austin Phelps, 1800s minister, educator, author

THE HISTORY OF PUBLISHING IN PICTURES

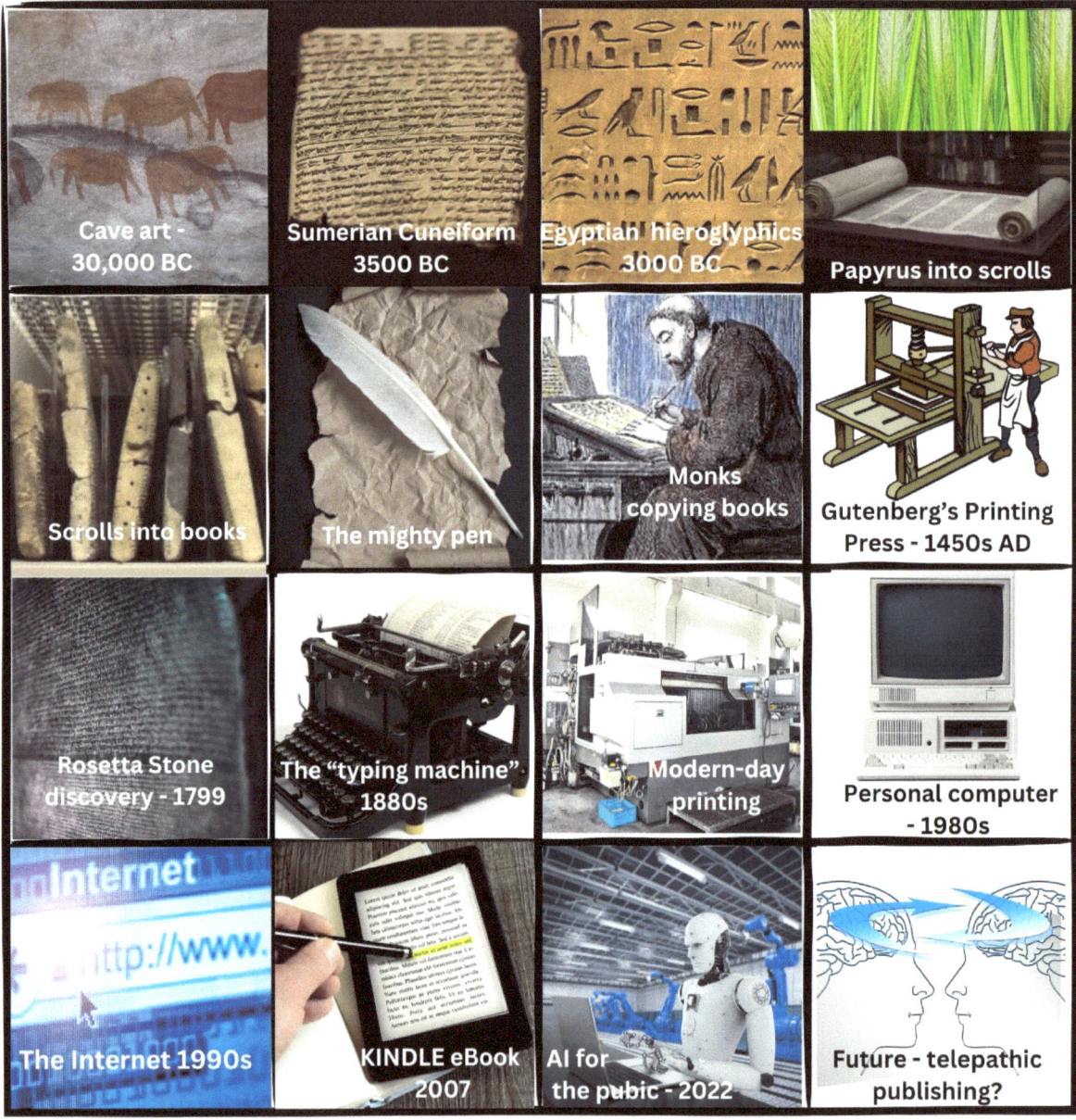

Cave art - 30,000 BC

Sumerian Cuneiform 3500 BC

Egyptian hieroglyphics 3000 BC

Papyrus into scrolls

Scrolls into books

The mighty pen

Monks copying books

Gutenberg's Printing Press - 1450s AD

Rosetta Stone discovery - 1799

The "typing machine" 1880s

Modern-day printing

Personal computer - 1980s

The Internet 1990s

KINDLE eBook 2007

AI for the pubic - 2022

Future - telepathic publishing?

PART I
ABOUT PUBLISHING

Photo: Sylvia Cary

"Life is either a daring adventure or it is nothing," — *Helen Keller*

PUBLISHING'S ROLLER-COASTER RIDE

As you can see from the previous page, "publishing" has had a long history. By the time the above photo was taken it 2018, this had become a common sight: *"Oh no, not another bookstore closing!?"* The game-changing Internet, POD technology, and Amazon had hit the traditional book industry hard.

When the pandemic came along in 2020, it looked like things would get worse for publishing, but instead it got better. As more people were forced to hunker down at home and do business online, they wrote more, read more, and ordered more books from online booksellers like Amazon. Sales went up. Writers got more time to write, and did. They flocked to self-publishing platforms, helping to shed most of the remaining stigma. It was now respectable. Authors who'd scoffed at self-publishing before now signed up. The next big disruption was the introduction of Artificial Intelligence (AI) to the general public in late 2022. Now it looks like authors can partner with AI to help them achieve their goal of "getting published" and can do so faster, cheaper, and more creatively than ever before.

"Publishing has changed in every way, how books look, how they're made, are sold, stored, priced, and read." —*Jonathan Kirsch, publishing attorney*

SIX PUBLISHING OPTIONS

There are basically six publishing options, so before you jump in, see what's out there. Consider the pros and cons of each. Make sure you're picking the best one for your specific book, talents, personality, and budget. Each option comes with its own set of rules.

Photo: CanvaPro

1. **TRADITIONAL PUBLISHING**
2. **MID-SIZE INDEPENDENT PUBLISHERS**
3. **ACADEMIC & UNIVERSITY PRESSES**
4. **HYBRIDS & AUTHOR SERVICE COMPANIES**
5. **SELF-PUBLISHING (AKA "INDIE")**
6. **INTERACTIVE ("SOCIAL") PUBLISHING**

Now, let's take a look at each option in more detail:

Photo: Berlin Publisher - CanvaPro

#1. TRADITIONAL PUBLISHING
[BIG 5 / NEW YORK / LEGACY / & IMPRINTS]

Summary: TRADITIONAL PUBLISHING in the US means targeting the big New York houses. The process is slow and competitive, and the odds for new authors are slim, but it's the gold standard for many, offering prestige and handling the bulk of the publishing process.

Traditional publishing is what most people think of when they hear the term "get published." Currently, the "Big Five" houses are Penguin Random House (PRH), Harper Collins, Simon & Schuster, Hachette Book Group, and Macmillan. Under the umbrella of each of the Big Five are their "imprints," many of them large enough so you've heard of them. If you are a new or new*ish* author, your chance of getting a book deal here, even with an agent, is only about 1-2% — but some people manage to do it.

How it Works: Typically, a traditional publisher buys/acquires ("acquisitions") a book manuscript, based on an author's book proposal (usually a must), submitted by the author's literary agent. If it's accepted, the author gets a book contract, deadline, and a cash "advance" (not all up front), theoretically to live on while finishing the book. Most authors need other sources of income to pay the bills.

Biggest Plus: Definitely it's the prestige, and the fact that the publisher pays an advance, takes the financial risk, and does the heavy lifting — the editing, design, formatting, proofing, cover, printing, distribution, and some (not all) of the marketing.

Biggest Minus: The amount of time it takes to get this far, and the number of gatekeepers along the way who can say NO. It can easily take 1-3 years.

#2. MID-SIZE INDEPENDENTS
[STAND-ALONE]

Photo: CanvaPro

Summary: MID-SIZE INDEPENDENTS are more accessible for newcomers, focusing on a variety of genres beyond bestsellers. They offer similar benefits to big publishers but you can expect smaller advances and less marketing support.

An "Independent" publishing house is not to be confused with the term "indie" publishing, which is another term for self-publishing. The *mid-size independents* function in the same way as the "Big Five," but are not under a Big Five umbrella. They are stand-alone and can be located anywhere. There are 100s of them. For newer authors who want to be traditionally published, these Independents are a more realistic option.

Biggest Plus: As with the Big Five, it's the prestige and getting the benefits of the publisher's expertise. While still considered "commercial," they may focus less on blockbusters penned by celebrity authors and more on areas of fiction, women's interest, memoirs, self-help, how-tos, children's books, and YA fare. Not one-size-fits-all. Study their websites.

Biggest Minus: Most likely you'll still need an agent. Even with one, the odds of a book deal are low with smaller advances and less marketing help.

#3. ACADEMIC, UNIVERSITY, & SMALL (MICRO) PRESSES

Illustration: CanvaPro

Summary: ACADEMIC & UNIVERSITY PRESSES mostly specialize in scholarly fields and may not require submission through an agent. They're prestigious and tend to move at a slow pace.

"Arrange the pieces that come your way."
– Virginia Wolfe

Not all academic and university publishers are stuffy. Some are quite mainstream. Many specialize in very specific areas, from art and baseball to the social sciences and travel. Check out each website individually for submission guideline. See which allow you to submit a book without an agent. You'll run into imprints such as Routledge, Norton, John Wiley, McGraw-Hill, New Harbinger, and the Chicken Soup books, as well as the university presses — Cambridge, Oxford, Princeton, and the presses for just about every state.

Biggest Plus: Once again, it's the prestige, the fact that you often don't need an agent, and the "street cred" you get, especially among your peers. In fact, if you are in a professional field (psychology, law, medicine) self-publishing might actually hurt you by getting you ignored. Consider this instead.

Biggest Minus: You can't be in a hurry. If you have a big conference presentation in six months and you want to sell your book, then self-publishing might be a safer way to go time-wise. Self-publishing for a ready-to-go book can be done in days, not years.

A REMINDER TO WRITE IT NOW

"Many people die with their music still in them. Why is this so? Too often it is because they are always getting ready to live. Before they know it, time runs out."
– Oliver Wendell Holmes

#4. HYBRIDS/AUTHOR ASSISTED
[BOOK DOCTORS / BOOK SHEPHERDS]

Photo: Ursula DiChito from Pixabay.com

Summary: HYBRIDS & AUTHOR SERVICES mix traditional support with self-publishing's autonomy. Authors pay for services, trading control for convenience but at a cost.

If you combine a dog with a horse, what do you get? Answer: *A "dorce."* In other words, a *hybrid.* In the book publishing world, a hybrid publisher theoretically combines the benefits of traditional publishing (you get help) with the benefits of self-publishing (you have more control). The hired hybrid publisher knows the ropes and does the bulk of the work, just as a traditional publisher does. But instead of getting an advance, the author pays for the help. Hopefully, the hybrid or book doctor doesn't accept "just anybody" who can pay, but honestly evaluates the work, and lets the writer know if their book is ready for publication, and if not, why not. Prices vary. Two better-known examples of hybrids are *Greenleaf* and *She Writes Press.* Google for more.

Photo: CanvaPro

Book Shepherds and Author Assisted companies are often tucked in between hybrid publishing and totally DIY self-publishing (see #5). You pay for help. You can pay outfits like *BookBaby.com* or *Lulu.com*, or individual book shepherds, book doctors, or publishing coaches who can offer more personalized help. Often these are editors with additional skills and know-how, who may also do cover design or formatting. As you can see, definitions can be fuzzy and there's lots of overlap.

Biggest Plus: The fact that an author doesn't have to go it alone – a big relief for those without the skills or interest in DIY publishing. For an overwhelmed writer, this may make the difference between getting published and not getting published. Hybrids and various types of paid helpers know what to do and possibly you don't, so it's worth it.

Biggest Minus: The cost. Plan to spend $1000s on the parts you need help with, usually the editing, proofreading, and cover.

Photo: Sylvia Cary

#5. SELF-PUBLISHING

[DIY/ KDP / INGRAMSPARK / BOOK COACHES]

Summary: The process of SELF-PUBLISHING puts you in charge, from all-DIY to hiring help for specific tasks. Platforms like KDP and IngramSpark offer expanded distribution free, but it requires a hands-on approach.

As of this writing, the 3 most popular *FREE* self-publishing platforms for paperback books and eBooks are:

1. *KDP (Kindle Direct Publishing)*;
2. *IngramSpark.com*, and;
3. *Draft-to-Digital (D2D.com)*.

Self-Publishing can mean doing every single bit of it all by yourself — writing, editing, proofreading, formatting, cover design, uploading, distributing, and marketing — to calling in a **Book Doctor/Coach** to partner with you, or join up with you just for specific tasks, like editing, proof-reading, or cover design. For names of freelancers, look at sites like *reedsy,com* and *janefriedman.com*, or check out freelancer sites like *fiverr.co*m or *Upwork.com*. The big difference between #1 and #2 above is *distribution.* While Amazon's KDP distributes just to Amazon sites around the world, IngramSpark distributes to 40,000 additional online booksellers worldwide, including Amazon, but they don't sell books directly from their own website. You still need Amazon for that. Draft-to-Digital is primarily an eBook formatter and distributor, but it also publishes paperbacks. It can get confusing!

Biggest Plus: When you self-publish, you are in control. No gatekeepers. You're the boss of it. If you've done the basics in terms of writing, producing, and marketing your self-published book, it has as good a chance of making sales. All FREE.

Biggest Minus: The *initial* perception on the part of many newbie authors that self-publishing is just "too hard" and "too complicated" to consider. True, there's a learning curve and the process has many bits and pieces, but they are learnable and doable. Once you've done it, it's a snap.

#6. INTERACTIVE "SOCIAL" PUBLISHING

Photo: CanvaPro

Summary: INTERACTIVE "SOCIAL" PUBLISHING on platforms like Wattpad, Medium, and Substack foster dIrect engagement with readers. It's a modern, gatekeeper-free approach, appealing for its quick feedback loop.

Ever imagine that you could have a writing career without paper? Or that you could publish your work before finishing it? Many writers are doing just this on such online publishing platforms as *Wattpad* and *RadishFiction.com*. What they like is the "engagement" with other writers and potential readers. By writing in public and getting feedback, users say they feel the process makes them better writers because they are dealing directly with the people who will be the ones buying their books.

Biggest Plus: Interactive publishing avoids the dreaded gatekeepers and eliminates the main obstacles, such as book proposals, agents, query letters, and endless wait times.

Biggest Minus: If you are social-media avoidant or want a physical book in your hand, this probably isn't the way to go, especially if you're not ready for "engagement." Use one of the other ways instead so you're still in your comfort zone.

A WORD ABOUT LITERARY AGENTS

"The key to success as an agent is not getting clients. That's easy. The key is knowing which publisher is going to like which book."
– Paul Levine, agent and attorney

If a publisher will only accept manuscript submissions through an agent, then you'll need to get an agent by sending them a book proposal (see next chapter). Once you get an agent (it can take months, if it happens at all), the benefits are many. Agents know what publishers are looking for, and they have personal contacts built up over years of networking. An agent may send your proposal out to dozens of publishers before selling it (no guarantees). See the end of this book for a list of websites to help you research AGENTS and other aspects of publishing.

WHAT TO CALL YOUR BOOK

Titles, like covers, are important. A good title can help sell a book; a bad one can help *sink* it. Don't connect your working title to an ISBN number too soon because if you want to CHANGE your title, you can't. You'll be stuck with it, or you'll have to buy a new ISBN. So hold off in case you change your mind about your title during the writing process. Sometimes just adding or changing a *sub*title does the trick.

WHICH OF THE SIX OPTIONS?

"When you get to a fork in the road, take it."
– Yogi Berra

Photo: Morguefile

DECISION TIME: Evaluate which publishing option best suits your book, skills, budget, and goals. Whether it's traditional, mid-size, academic, hybrid, self-publishing, or interactive social publishing, it's all up to you. Your choice will shape your publishing journey. If you choose the wrong one, no worries. You can back up and start again.

PART II
WRITING YOUR BOOK

"The hardest part of writing is knowing what to write."
    – Syd Field, author and screenwriter

Photo: CanvaPro

WHAT TO WRITE ABOUT

If You Are Undecided, Here's a 3-Part Exercise:

Part 1: The 5-Minute Test:

On a file card, write down **3 things** you know something about, are good at, or have interest in, such as work, an avocation, a hobby, cause, a concern, period in history, question, speculation, theory, or place. Mull them over. Can you see yourself spending a year living with this topic? Will you lose interest or lose steam? **Pick one** of your three – the one that most resonates with you. Put a check mark by it. Consider that your book's *working topic*. Do you want to write about this topic as fiction, memoir, or non-fiction? Or maybe as a narrative non-fiction book with dialogue and description?

Part 2: The 5-Hour Test:

Now that you've got your topic and genre, do 4 hours of research using these 4 websites, *one hour on each:*

a. *Amazon.com* – Search for other books on your topic, especially those published in the last 5 years. These are your "comps" (competition);
b. *Wikipedia* – get a birds-eye overview of your topic. Is your topic bigger than you thought?
c. *Google* your topic to see what's available. Get a sense of how "hot" it is – or *not*.
d. *YouTube* – Who is talking about your topic? Any podcasts or gurus? Any new aspects? News?

During the 5th hour, using your new knowledge, write a "faux" Table of Contents for your book, even if it's fiction or memoir. 12 total chapters. You can divide it into 2 or 3 parts if you wish. Figure out how much territory your book will cover. If it's a memoir or personal-experience book, your research may include journals, letters, blogs, and fact-checking, so substitute *that* for one of the above sites.

Part 3: The 5-Day Test

Write a first draft of your *first chapter* in your book, whether it's fiction, a memoir, or non-fiction. Each genre has its own challenges. First chapters need to whet the reader's appetite so they want to keep on reading. By the time you've completed this part of the test, you'll probably know whether or not you want this to be your final topic choice. If what you learned from this 3-part exercise is that the topic doesn't work for you, then go back to the drawing board. Keep going until you finally know what you want to write about.

WHAT'S YOUR WRITING GOAL?

"No wind favors a ship without a destination." — *Seneca*

Not every author aspires to becoming a best-seller, even though it sounds good. You may not want the busy lifestyle or time-commitment that can go along with being a success. Some authors just want to publish a book to give them "street cred" for teaching and speaking engagements. Others want to publish a collection of photos, poems, or recipes to share with friends and family. Or write a memoir as a legacy for their future generations. A mental health professional might want a book for their clients to help them deal with a specific issue. You don't need to be a best-seller to do *any* of these things. Identifying your publishing goals up front can save you a lot of time, money, and stress.

Photo: Pixabay

THE *REAL* RESEARCH FOR YOUR BOOK

Your initial research was to help you pick your topic and get you started. Now that you know what you want to write about, know your writing goal, and know the *scope* of your book (as detailed in your faux Table of Contents), the real job of research begins, the kind that will make your book stand out from other books, even those on the same topic. Revisit the four websites in the exercise. On *Amazon.com*, pick out five books like yours from the last five years, your "comps." Look inside them. Read customer comments or reviews. However, if you are writing a memoir, narrative non-fiction, or novel, your new research might be reading your old journals, looking at photo albums, or finding a couple of experts on your topic online and following them. Consult with AI for research suggestions. Add the sites and podcasts of experts and thought leaders on your topic.

LET THE TYPING BEGIN. . .

How are you physically planning to write your book? Longhand on a yellow lined pad? By going straight to the computer? By dictating it into your phone and transcribing it later? Or are you going to wing it and just start typing to see what happens? Also, do you want to pre-format the manuscript to the trim size you want (such as 6 by 9 inches) so you know the page count as you go along? You can do these things. And *where* will you write? At a desk? Comfy chair?

AVOIDING KILLER INTERRUPTIONS

The late self-publishing guru Dan Poynter once quoted novelist Judith Krantz, who is said to have placed this sign on her office door when writing:

**"DO NOT COME IN.
DO NOT SAY HELLO.
DO NOT SAY 'I'M LEAVING.'
DO NOT SAY ANYTHING
UNLESS THE HOUSE IS ON FIRE."**

NAILING YOUR BOOK'S ANGLE & THEME

"My kingdom for a horse" *--King Richard III*

No matter what your topic or genre, getting the right story angle, hook, or intended message can be hard. For example, you can't just write "about war" or "about love." Those topics are too big. You need an angle, just like King Richard needed a horse: *"My kingdom for an angle!"* An angle for a novel about divorce (another big topic) might be telling the tale from the point of view of the child. Even harder is understanding the *theme*, what the book is really about aside from the details. Themes are often stated in abstract terms: *war is hell; honesty pays; love heals,* and so on. An author may not be sure what their book is about until they've finished it. "Ah, it's about *redemption!* I just realized that!" When your A*ha!* Moment about your theme finally hits you, the writing suddenly becomes a lot easier.

HOW LONG SHOULD A BOOK BE?

Photo: CanvaPro

"60-80,000 words is a gorgeous word count."
— Amy Collins, New Shelves Books

ABOUT WORDAGE
One page, double-spaced, is about 250 words
One page, single-spaced is about 500 words
Children's picture book – 32 pages (# words varies)
Regular Short story 2,000-5,000+ words
Magazine feature article 2,500-7,500 words

Novella 17,500-40,000 words
Novel 50,000-100,000 (#WGA) words
Commercial fiction 80,000-90,000 words
Dissertation 100-200 pages (25,000-50,000 words)
Screenplay 120 pages (# words not important)
New Yorker **magazine article – 2,000-10,000 words**

A Famous 6-Word Short Story:

"For Sale. Baby Shoes. Never Worn."
– *Ernest Hemingway*

WHO IS YOUR BOOK'S AUDIENCE?

Wall art in Hollywood by Tom Suriya called "You Are the Star"

Some audiences for a book are obvious. A book on parenting is intended for parents. But most books have more than one audience. A book on parenting might also be of interest to psychotherapists who treat parents in therapy, or to teachers who need parenting skills in the classroom, even if they aren't themselves parents. You can go hunting for readers where they are, or you can let readers find you ("discoverability"). The stronger the reader's need for the information you offer in your book, the more likely they'll find you, especially if you've picked good *keywords* and *categories* on the KDP form, have a good cover, and wrote a good book description on for your Amazon book page. Try to come up with at least *three* possible audiences for your book. Research "audiences." Ask yourself, *Who should read my book, even if they don't want to? What's in it for them?* ("reader benefits"). *What hobby or professional groups do they belong to?* What are their *pain points*? Make **lists.** Market to them.

WHY BOOK PROPOSALS ARE GOOD FOR YOU

12 Basic Book Proposal Elements

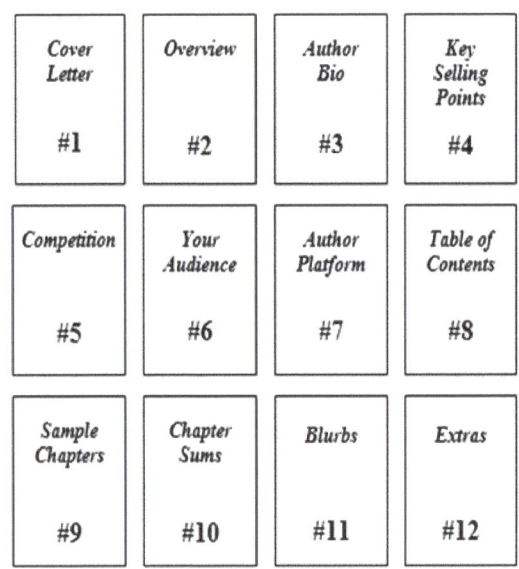

Graphic: Common Elements of a Book Proposal – by Sylvia Cary

ELEMENTS OF A BOOK PROPOSAL

A book proposal is usually a requirement for playing in the *traditional* publishing game, but not always in academia or if using a smaller press. Still, a book proposal is a useful tool to help you organize and structure your book, so consider writing one anyway.

Cover letter – the letter you include to the agent introducing yourself and your book proposal.

Overview (synopsis) - two pages double-spaced. Tells what book is about, including the ending.

Author bio/photo – add something unique to your bio and a professional but "warm" photo.

Key Selling Points – a bullet-point list of what's special and unique about the book and the author.

Competition ("comps") – list 5 competitive books and state how is your book is better and different? What are its added values?

Audience – What groups (business leaders? Moms?) are likely to want/need to read your book?

Author Platform – Why should anyone buy a book by you? Are you a name in your field? Have a following? Winner of any awards?

Table of Contents for book – tells what's in each chapter, and what territory is covered in the book.

Sample Chapters – Usually two, one from the beginning, and a later one fulfilling book's promise.

Chapter Summaries – A paragraph or two summarizing what's in each chapter, except for the two full-length chapters you are already sending.

Blurbs & Extras - Any magazine or newspaper articles about you? Awards? Recognitions?

Extras: Can add anything special that's related to book - an article, report, or topic-related research.

Front Matter: Title page, Copyright page, Dedication; Table of Contents, Foreword, Preface, Introduction.

Middle Matter – the book's content, including divider pages, photos, graphics, "call-outs," etc.

Back Matter – About the Author, Also by. Resources, index, footnotes, Letter from author to readers, etc.

Cash Cow Alert! Self-publishing has brought scammers out of the woodwork. Be wary of anyone who says they can get you a book deal, make your book into a best-seller, or get your book adapted into a movie. They prey on indie authors who are new to the publishing world, and don't know how things work. Consult Writer Beware listed under SFWA.org (Science Fiction Writers of America) for warnings.

5 THINGS WRITERS WORRY ABOUT

Photo: CanvaPro

"Ideas are everywhere. It's the execution that's difficult." — Joanna Penn, thecreativepenn.com

1. Should I copyright my book IDEA? You can't copyright an idea, no matter how brilliant. Ideas are in the air. Ideas are up for grabs. What counts is how you express your idea. If you present it in a fresh way, it will help your book stand out. If someone steals your actual words, that's plagiarism.

2. Should I copyright my book TITLE? Same answer: You can't copyright titles either. For example, many

people have used the title "The Gift." The exception is "trademarking." So check your working title idea with the U.S. Trademark Office (uspto.gov). However, in most cases you can use the same title as somebody else, but why would you want to? It's a marketing nightmare. To stand out, pick a new title.

3. Can I write about real people in my life?
Yes, but there's an art to it. You probably won't get sued for saying something nice about somebody, but if you need to say something unflattering or embarrassing about another, then learn *the art of disguise*. Changing names isn't enough. Change all identifying characteristics. Or get signed permission.

4. Can I Quote Other People in my Book?
This is in the area of "fuzzy law." Under the legal protection of "Fair Use," authors are permitted to use *limited* quotes from other sources in their own writings with proper attributions. This applies to quoting from books, articles, journals, and speeches, but not from song lyrics and poetry. Here, it's risky, depending on the work being quoted from. You may need to get legal permission from the copyright owner. Each case may be different. Tread carefully.

5. What if I do/don't get famous? In most cases, you won't be burdened with fame and fortune, *nor* will you have a humiliating, public fail. Half of first-time authors sell an average of only 200 books, whether *self* or traditionally published. Most writing careers take more than one book, so keep writing. Learn on the job. Success may creep up on you.

"I've always been famous. It's just no one knew it yet." – Lady Gaga

BOOK EDITING ROCKS!

"The difference between the right word and *almost* the right work is like the difference between lightning and lightning bug."

– Mark Twain

TYPES OF BOOK EDITING

"Edit or you'll get hammered." – Rick Smith

Photo: CanvaPro

Home Editing: Do as much editing on your own as you can. Read and re-read your pages. Read aloud for timing and flow. Run chapters through any built-in spell-checker or grammar-checker. They catch a lot. Smooth out sentences. Do this often.

Editing with Tools: Both Grammarly.com and ProWritingAid.com have free versions. Do the small stuff, like fixing wayward comas, with a free tool, and then let a paid editor do the big stuff, like structure.

Artificial Intelligence: As AI gets more powerful and capable of handling larger files (such as a full book), it will probably become the "editor" and "proofreader" of choice for authors. Stay tuned.

A Professional Book Evaluation: Before hiring a book editor to EDIT your book, have them do a book evaluation first (no editing) to see if your book is even ready for editing and, if so, which kind?

STANDARD BOOK EDITING PHASES

"The first draft of anything is shit." *– Hemingway*

1. Developmental (Substantive) Editing: Mostly looks at the Big Picture – the structure, organization, style, potential, and promises to the reader. Is the book idea viable? What's needed to make it work?

2. Line editing - The focus here is on the language, writing style, clarity, and flow, which may mean scrambling sentences/pages around for readability.

3. Copy editing - Details are now in the spotlight – grammar, spelling, punctuation, repeated words, phrasing, formatting, inconsistencies, and hyphens. If fiction: characters, plot, names, descriptions, reader experience, and appropriate use of research.

4. Proofreading (overlaps with above) The final editorial pass before the book goes to press to catch goofs – from typos, to header mistakes, to extra blank pages. It's a very important form of nitpicking.

PART III
PUBLISHING YOUR BOOK

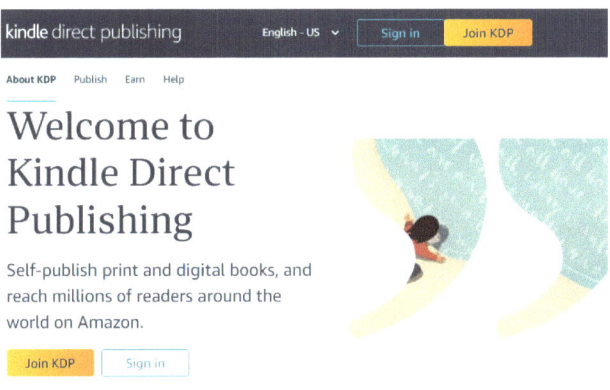

When you first sign up for a self-publishing platform, like Amazon's KDP, it can take a while to wrap your head around the idea that "self-publishing" means that *you* are in charge of everything. You may think of Amazon as your "publisher," but Amazon is really your printer. *You're* the publisher. You're the one who tells KDP what to do and when to do it. The actual publishing part just involves uploading two pdf files to KDP – your book, and your cover.

SIGNING UP FOR KDP

To get things rolling, go to:

kdp.amazon.com

Sign up with an email address and a password. If you're already an Amazon customer, you can use that email and password. Sign up *before* you finish writing your book so you can get familiar with the site and start filling things out. (FYI, KDP used to be called CreateSpace).

Once you sign up, you'll be taken to the **Bookshelf Page.** This is where all the excitement takes place. It's the HUB. You'll probably be popping in and out of here a lot.

Later on, when you are ready to start working on a book (or new book), click on the + Create button:

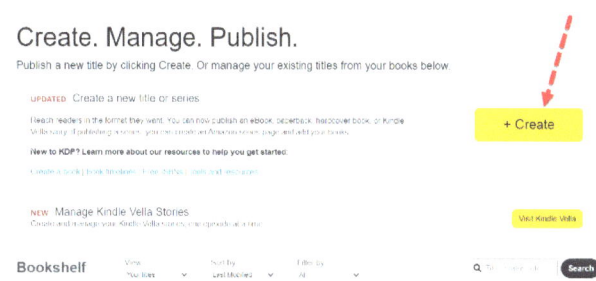

EXPLORING THE KDP NEIGHBORHOOD

Poke around a little. Explore the neighborhood. If you want to take a deeper dive, there are video tutorials on the site as well as on *YouTube.com.* There's enough to read and watch about self-publishing on Amazon to keep you busy for days.

THE IMPORTANT 3 DOTS (. . .)

After you type in your new book title, look over on the right and you'll see 3 dots (. . .) referred to as "THE ELLIPSIS." These dots are important. CLICK on them. You get a menu. What's on the menu changes according to where you are in the publishing process. The menu answers many of your questions, such as, *"How do I fill in the KDP form?"* or *"How do I change the wording of my book description?"* or *"How do I order proof copies?"* or *"How do I buy my own book?"*

SAMPLE ELLIPSIS MENU ***

Edit print book details
Edit print book content
Edit print book pricing
Request Printed Proofs
Order author copies
Promote and Advertise

Archive title
Add to series
Unpublish print book
Unlink Books

YOUR BOOK'S PUBLISHING "IMPRINT"

When the KDP form asks you for your publisher's name (imprint), remember, that means you. You are your own publishing company, so give it a nice name. To make sure that the imprint name you pick isn't already taken, first Google it, then check it out on the website of the U.S. Trademark Office (*uspto.gov*). The *uspto.gov* site is FREE and not complicated. Just watch out for pop-up ads. Don't sign up for anything by mistake. You don't need to. Just follow the instructions to get the information you need.

The Size & Shape of Your Book (Trim Size):

Choosing the trim size of your book is fun. There are so many options. You are not stuck with a typical 6x9-inch shape. It can be bigger, smaller, shorter, taller, square, oblong, paperback, hardcover, or just a digital eBook, in black and white or color, on cream paper, white paper, or a special paper for photos, with a glossy or matte cover finish. Look at your own books at home, or go to a bookstore and measure the books you like. To check out available trim sizes, go to: **kdp.amazon.com/trimsize**

A HEADS UP: THE KDP FORM

Don't be fooled by the easy-peasy looking initial questions and on the kdp form and figure you can just breeze through it to get it over with. Your answers are more important than you think. They will influence book sales. More on this later.

PRE-WRITING YOUR BOOK DESCRIPTION

For example: When you get to the part on the KDP form where you are asked to write a **book description**, it doesn't look important, but it IS important. It's going to end up on the Amazon website next to your book cover when your book is published! It's what potential customers will read before deciding whether or not to buy your book. The book description needs to be good. Enticing. It's your main sales pitch. You'll be using it a lot for marketing.

A book description should be aimed at your specific audience(s). What does your audience need and want in life that can be obtained by reading your book? If your book description addresses a reader's need, want, or problem, they'll buy.

To Research Book Descriptions: Start by reading the advice KDP offers, then search for articles and blogs on *"How to write a book description,"* or watch a couple of *YouTube* tutorial or podcasts, or consult the websites and blogs of the current self-publishing gurus for advice. Since you get a maximum of 4000 characters (not words), use them. Publishing industry expert Jane Friedman (*janefriedman.com*) advises placing your best "pitch" at the beginning of your book description before Amazon cuts it off with their "Read More" line. Use a blurb or create a logline at the top. Use bullet points to draw attention to a list of important topics in the book, then include a short bit about the *benefits to the reader* (super important), then end with suggestions for who *should* buy this book. Is it for "new moms," "dog lovers," or maybe "mental health professionals?" Finally, cut and paste your edited and proofed book description into the KDP description box.

PRE-WRITING YOUR AUTHOR BIO

You'll use an author bio often during the marketing phase, different lengths for different occasions, including on your Author Central Page on Amazon (see Part IV on MARKETING). If you don't have a website, then your Author Central page on Amazon, with its own URL, will do.

Don't write a dry, boring bio. Let readers know you. Put in something memorable. What's unique in your background? Born in an unusual place (a bookstore?) or during an unusual circumstance? (a tornado?). Grow up in a special situation? Educated or trained in a special area? (law, art, medicine?) Had any interesting jobs or life experiences? (ex-cop or CIA?) Include a few talking points and facts that aren't in a typical bio. *Who* you are is important to your readers.

ABOUT GETTING YOUR ISBN(s)

An ISBN (International Standard Book Number) is unique to each published book and is used world-wide. The official ISBN agency for the U.S. is *Bowker.com*. Other countries have their own ISBN systems. If you self-publish through KDP, you get 3 options:

The 3 ISBN Options:

1. A FREE ISBN which can be used only on Amazon;
2. An ISBN you've already bought in from Bowker *myidentifiers.com*. (Currently the cost on Bowker is 1

for $125 or a 10-pack for $295). CLICK on "*Bring my own.*"

3. Buy an ISBN through KDP at a discount. CLICK on "*Bring my own,*" and then KDP takes you to the *myidentifiers.com* website to get your discount. Cost is currently $99. Your ISBN should appear in a window next to the 3 options listing. Cut and paste it onto your desktop or elsewhere for safe-keeping.

RESEARCHING YOUR 7 KEYWORDS

Photo CanvaPro

A "keyword" in Amazon-speak isn't *literally* one single word, it can be a short phrase or "word string" up to 50 characters (spaces count as characters). "Keywords" are the words that potential customers may type into the Amazon search window when they're looking for a book but they don't know the title, or the author, or even if such a book exists.

Here's your chance to help them "discover" YOUR book. If they type in the same words you've predicted they'll type in – it's a match! Your book could pop up in the customer's search results. The higher up your book is on the search results list, the better the chances are they'll buy it.

To test out your keywords, type them into the Amazon search window one word or phrase at a time. If a menu pops up, look through it to see if your word or phrase is there. If it is, great! Definitely keep that word or phrase as one of your 7 keywords on your KDP form. If there are no matches, it means nobody else is using that search term, so pick another one and test it out the same way. For more on the art and science of keyword hunting, look on *YouTube* or check out Dave Chesson's *PublisherRocket.com*, which has a one-time fee, then it's yours.

Photo: CanvaPro

PICKING YOUR BASIC 3 CATEGORIES

Amazon's millions of books and eBooks are categorized. Your book probably fits into more than one category. KDP asks you to pick 3 basic categories under which to list your book. This gives you a chance to be a "best-seller" in three categories. Your book's categories inform potential book buyers about the book's primary genre, and where it would be shelved in a bookstore or library. On the categories part of the KDP form, each time you CLICK on one of the categories listed, additional sub-menus open up so you can zero in on what best described your book, making it easier for customers to get exactly what they are looking for.

5 WRITING TIPS

1. Even if you're an expert at something, write conversationally. Avoid psychobabble, legalese, and insider-speak. Instead, *communicate*.
2. Don't over-quote experts. It's your book. If you want to come across as an expert, quote yourself.
3. Research what's already been done. Who has been down this road before? Take it from there.
4. Are you a linear or top-down writer? A morning or night writer? Factor this in to your writing schedule.
5. The secret of writing is writing. The more you write, the better you get, the easier it becomes.

HOW TO MAKE A BOOK COVER

Self-published authors get to have a say-so about their book covers. Most traditionally published authors don't. By the time they get to see their cover, it's a done deal, or they may get a chance to pick one of two, maybe three, mock-ups.

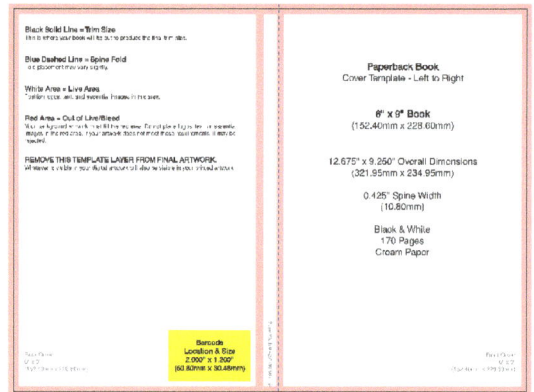

Typical book cover template for a standard-size 6x9-inch trim book with 170 pages, on cream paper. The number of pages determines the width of the spine. Cream paper is thicker than white paper.

Search for *"kdp.amazon.com/cover-calculator."*

PHOTOS & GRAPHICS

Of course, you'll want something nice to put on your book cover, probably art or a photo. To get these free without restrictions on commercial use, check out sites like **Pixabay.com, Visualhunt.com, Canva.com**, and some others.

TO DIY OR GET COVER DESIGN HELP

In the past, hiring a graphic designer to do a cover for your book was pricey, but today there are a number of sites where cover design help is budget friendly, among them *fiverr.com*, *99Design.com*, *upwork.com*, and *blog.reedsy.com*.

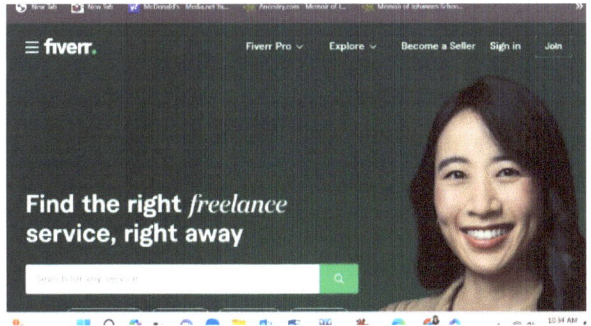

Fiverr.com: An international website for freelancers, including book cover designers, artists, writers, marketers, and more.

BOOK COVERS FOR DIY-ERS

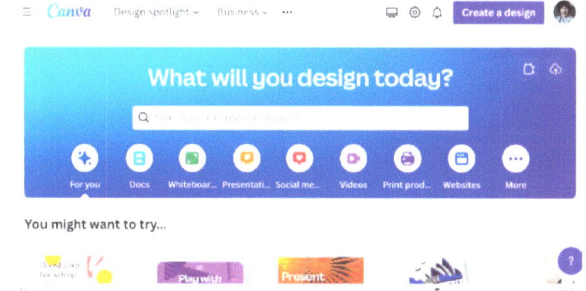

Canva.com website for graphic design - free & paid versions

With the exploding field of Artificial Intelligence, there are an increasing number of new apps with text-to-pictures capabilities. Think of it as "verbal design." Search for the latest sites to help you create a beautiful cover.

ABOUT E-BOOKS

Photo: CanvaPro

Can you publish *just* an eBook and not the paperback? *Yes.* And with an eBook you'll still be a "published author." You'll have a book page on Amazon along with an Amazon Author Page (see Part IV on MARKETING). You can start with Amazon's formatting platform, Kindle Create (see next page), and then go on to the Draft2Digital site and use their formatting tools. If you need assistance, you can hire formatting help through sites like *reedsy.com*, *upwork.com* or *fiverr.com*.

The **Upside** of publishing just an eBook is the speed of production and distribution.

21

The *Downside* is the fact that a paperback has more prestige. Consider doing both, or at least printing up a few paperback copies for show.

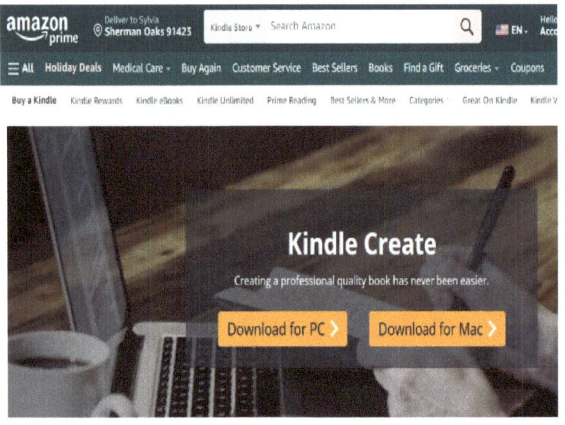

For broader distribution, check out Draft2Digital (see site photo below).

D2D or *Draft2Digital.com* is FREE and has formatting instructions plus customer support. As mentioned earlier, it's primarily an eBook distributor, but also publishes paperback books and eBooks.

PREVIEWER & PROOF COPIES

On KDP, before you can officially CLICK on the "Approve" publication button, there's one more step**: The KDP "Previewer."** It allows you to see on your computer screen exactly what your book will look like when published. It gives you a chance to spot mistakes - such as a missing page number or an extra blank page. Then it's strongly recommended that you order a physical **proof copy** of your book. Seeing your book in person prior to publication makes a huge difference.

WRITE IT. EDIT IT. PROOF IT. FIX IT.
APPROVE IT. NOW PUBLISH IT.

Once you have been through the above steps you can finally CLICK on **"Publish."** Amazon tells you that you may have to wait a few days for your book to appear on the Amazon site, but sometimes it's just a few hours. To check, go online to *Amazon.com* (CLICK on "Books" on the drop-down menu) and type in your book title. At first, you may have to also have to type in your author name until the algorithm gets to know you. Seeing your book cover there on Amazon is an *exciting moment*. After publication, register your copyright at copyright.gov (see below).

FINISHING ENERGY QUOTE
"Done is better than perfect."
– Mark Zuckerberg

NOW YOU'RE PUBLISHED AT LAST!

PART IV
MARKETING YOUR BOOK

"Writing is only half the task. The other half is getting your work into the hands of readers"
– Jerry B. Jenkins, author and publisher

Photo: CanvaPro

There's a little bit a heartbreak in every published book. *– Sylvia Cary*

After the initial excitement of finally "getting published," there can be a letdown, a kind of *post-publication depression* that sets it which usually isn't expected. It can be triggered by a small thing, such as a friend saying they're going to order your book from Amazon right away and then not doing it, or sending a gift copy to somebody and not hearing back. These are the little heartbreaks we hide because admitting to disappointment is embarrassing. Just know many of us have experienced the same thing and understand. Anyone who has ever published a book has been there. It passes. Book marketing helps. . .

. . .At least, book marketing can't hurt!

"My first book didn't sell because I didn't promote it." - Former President Bill Clinton

Photo: Sylvia Cary

You have got to toot your own horn!

15 WAYS TO SHOW YOUR BOOK EXISTS
- **#1.** Launch Day Email Announcement
- **#2.** Emails to Your Lists
- **#3.** One-and-Done
- **#4.** Handouts
- **#5** "Amazon World"
- **#6.** "Going Wide" / Double Publish
- **#7.** Website or Landing Page
- **#8.** Social Media
- **#9.** Book Reviews
- **#10** Contests
- **#11.** Bookstores & Libraries
- **#12** SEO Article Writing
- **#13** Speaking
- **#14.** Networking
- **#15.** Your Next Book

DISCOVERABILITY

"You can't sell a book if no one knows it exists." *—Said by just about everybody*

Photo CanvaPro

When you're a new or still relatively unknown author, the secret of success is "discoverability" which means a potential book buyer, who may never have heard of you and has no idea that your book exists, can still find you and buy your book. How does *that* happen? The answer is, it happens because you did these 3 things right:

- You wrote a good book which facilitated *word-of-mouth* marketing;
- You produced a professional-looking product; and;
- You marketed your book by trying a number of different marketing ideas (mutual funds style), instead of putting all your eggs in one basket, like a single paid display ad that might not pay off for you.

In a 2023 podcast, self-publishing expert Joanna Penn (*TheCreativePenn.com*) said there are currently about 15 million books on Amazon, up from a mere *half* a million a decade ago. With that much competition, how are you ever going to get a book-buyer's attention for *your* book? Getting it into bookstores isn't the answer. It *was* the answer once, but not now when 70% of sales are *online*, not in bookstores. So, whether we like it or not, it looks like we're stuck with "book marketing." True, nobody *has* to market their book. It's not a law. You can *publish-it-and-forget-it* if you want, but then you won't sell many books.

Here are **15 Ways to Show Your Book Exists.** They can be tackled in order, so you don't have to keep stopping to figure out what you should do next.

#1. LAUNCH DAY EMAIL ANNOUNCEMENT

If you don't do at least *something* to commemorate your official "Launch Day" when your book is first available for sale, the day may slip by and it will feel just like any other day. Send out a short email to people you know *personally* (friends, family, neighbors, work colleague – whatever feels appropriate) announcing your exciting news. Do this even if your list is only ten people. You have to start somewhere. Keep this email simple:

> Hi All,
> I'm excited to announce the publication of my new book *(novel/ non-fiction book memoir/children's book)* called _____ *(title/subtitle)*. It's about _____.
> Here's the link to the book on Amazon *(cut and paste link here)*. I'd love it if you'd check it out.

Sign it and embed or attach your book cover image and link to it on Amazon. To get the book link, go to your

Amazon book page, highlight and copy the long link that's in the search window, and paste it into your email. To shorten it, use *bitly.com* or *tinyurl.com*.

2. EMAIL TO YOUR OTHER LISTS

Now is the time to email the rest of your world to say you've published a book. You can use the same letter as above, or maybe make it a bit more formal. Most of us have contacts beyond friends and family – an extended Christmas card list, members of groups, organizations, and associations we belong to, writing group members, neighborhood lists, and alumni lists. These are people who've signed up for hearing from you in one way or another and won't consider your launch letter "spam." (Don't forget to include that link to your Amazon book page. Make it easy for people to buy your book). Speaking of *lists*, there are other lists to create for other kinds of book marketing, such as bloggers, podcasters, publications, bookstores, libraries. Also collect relevant hashtags for social media posts. *Google* and AI (*ChatGPT*) are good for lists.

#3. ONE-AND-DONE

Some marketing actions take only minutes and need to be done only once. Some work for you in the background while you're doing other things:

A 30-Second Elevator Pitch: If somebody asks you, *"What's your book about?"* have a good answer *memorized*. Write it on a file card   to keep handy. Include the genre, title, who the book is for, a benefit, and where it can be bought.

Class Notes: Are you a graduate of an educational institution? Nursery school? Grade school? High school? College? Grad school? Specialty school? Dance class? Fencing academy? Gun club?

Gr

Graphic: Carrie Booth from Pixabay

Well, send an email about your book to their newsletter editor or "Class Notes" section. People like to read what former classmates are up to.

Email Signature Block: Create a little ad for your book at the bottom of every email you send. Include a book cover image and link to your Amazon book page, website, or blog if you have them. This isn't aggressive, in-your-face selling. It's subtle. Your ad just sits there minding its own business, and people can click on the links if interested—or not. Google for a "How-To" about setting this up for your particular email service.

HARO: This 4-letter word stands for "Help a Reporter Out." *HARO.com* sends you daily or weekly emails with requests from reporters, authors, researchers, bloggers, and members of the media who need a quick answer to a question or want a quote from an expert on a specific topic. Answer and explain why you're an expert. It's good PR, and it's doing a service for a colleague. It lasts for years unless you opt out.

Google Alert: The modern equivalent of a clipping service. Sign up to get an email alert whenever Google finds your name or finds something you've specified that's related to your book title or topic.

#4. HANDOUTS

Printed materials or "handouts" are still a good way to spread the word about your book, either in person, by snail mail, or digitally. Use local printers, or Google for online printers, like *VistaPrint.com*. Pick your **brand colors** by uploading your book cover to a graphic design site like *Canva.com* (free and fee) and it will create a color palette for you. Use those colors for your marketing pieces so they all tie together. People will start to think of you when they see those color combos. You can create *business cards, postcards, bookmarks, flyers, brochures, one-sheets*, even *postage* stamps. Include what fits without looking squished: book cover image, author photo, logline, blurbs, review snippet, author's website URL and, of course, where to buy the book.

#5. AMAZON WORLD

Photo: CanvaPro

While the term "Amazon World" may sound like a theme park, it's a good way for authors to remember that Amazon has a lot to offer authors to help them sell books. For example:

a. **Your Amazon Book Page:** Once your book is published, it appears LIVE on certain Amazon sites around the world. That's pretty amazing. You can LOOK INSIDE the book as well as read the back cover, just as you would in a bookstore.

b. **Personal Author Central Page:** This is like having your own webpage or landing page right on Amazon. To get access, go to *author.amazon.com* and follow the directions for fixing up the page to your liking. You can upload your bio, headshot, as well as covers from other published books.

c. **Customer Reviews / Comments** – Beg people for these! Some authors ask for Customer Reviews at the end of their book. Customer comments help potential buyers decide whether (or not) to buy your book. The more reviews, the better. Scroll down to "Write a Review" for directions.

e. **Foreign Amazon Sites:** Think globally. Your book will be on many foreign Amazon sites, so check them out. A list is given on your Author Central page. Make sure you fill this page out.

f. **A+ Content Display Ad**. You can create a FREE display ads on your Amazon book page. There's a learning curve involved. Access instructions through your KDP bookshelf page. CLICK on the 3 dots. (...) Pick "promote and advertise" on the menu.

g. **Paid Ads**: This is probably something you should hold off on until you're a more experienced book marketer. Watch *YouTube* tutorials on "ads."

h. **Video:** Amazon gives you an opportunity to video pitch your book. From your book page, scroll down to "Videos" then CLICK on "Upload Your Video." An author's "personal human touch" is important and helps sell books.

#6. "GOING WIDE" / DOUBLE PUBLISHING

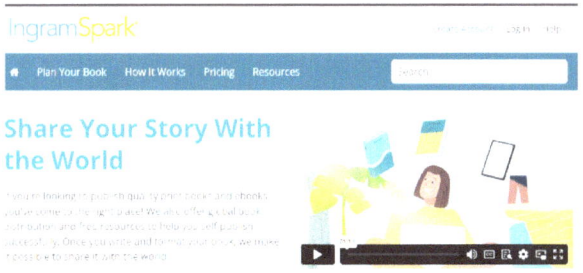

IngramSpark self-publishing website

As stated earlier, Amazon has about 70% of the online retail market. Many Amazon authors are content with just that. However, if you want your book to be distributed to the other 30% of online booksellers around the globe (such as Barnes & Noble, Powell Books, and some 40,000 other digital marketplaces), the best way to do that is to publish your paperback a second time on the *IngramSpark.com* self-publishing platform – referred to as "double publishing" or "going wide." It's FREE, just more work, but it gets you listed in the Ingram catalog which bookstores get. A customer should be able to walk into a bookstore and order your book, even though it's not physically in the store. To "go wide" with your eBook, start with Amazon's Kindle, then sign up with the previously mentioned *D2D.com* (*Draft2Digital.com*), which will make your eBook available for iTunes, Apple, Nook, Kobo, and other eBook marketplaces. Authors can format their eBook on the D2D site. Free ISBNs.

#7. WEBSITE OR LANDING PAGE

As the author of a published book, you need to be findable. What if somebody from the media wants to interview you, or a group wants you to speak? At least you have your Author Central Page on Amazon with its own URL, but you should also have your own personal website or landing page with the basics on it – book cover image, book synopsis, contact information, author bio and photo, blurbs, review snippets, and where your book can be bought. You can hire help (*blog.reedsy.com, fiverr.com, upwork.com*) or DIY (*Canva.com, WordPress, Wix, Weebly*, or *SquareSpace*). Your domain name can be your own name (or a variation), or your book's title (or a variation), such as "*booktitlethenovel*.com."

#8. SOCIAL MEDIA

You don't have to do it all! If you're not already active on social media, then just stick your toe in the water with one or two platforms that have something about them that appeals to you, like photos. In that case, Instagram is a good choice. Or Pinterest. Follow a few people; lurk awhile before sharing. See how the others do it. With some, the usual "best practices" advice is to make 80% of your posts *non*-marketing, and only 20% about your book. There's plenty of help available here. Search *YouTube*. Consult AI's ChatGPT (or other AI sites) for step-by-step directions on use.

#9. BOOK REVIEWS

What's a book without a book review, right? They seem to go together like bacon and eggs. Book reviews influence book buyers to buy, plus they're a good source of blurbs for marketing. Sadly, many book review resources (such as newspapers) have disappeared. One popular substitute is the online book blogger book review. To get lists, try:

📖 *Google.com (ask for list of book bloggers)*
📖 *AI - ChatGPT.com (prompt for book bloggers)*
📖 *BookBloggerList.com*
📖 *Reedsy.com/discovery (can get paid-for review)*
📖 *Midwestbookreview.com (fee for review / lists)*

#10. CONTESTS

A win, place, or show in a writing contest makes you an "award-winning author" which pulls you out of the crowd of 1000s of newly published authors. It's good for book marketing. It's something you can write a press release or a blog post about. It's another photo op: Take a picture of the award or gold sticker. Get lists of contests and check out their reputations. Make sure they are respectable. They don't have to be the top contests, but watch out for scams. Search below for "writing contests" and "best writing contests" to weed out the baddies:

📖 *Blog.Reedsy.com (500 contests)*
📖 *janefriedman.com (has contest information)*
📖 *JerryJenkins.com (lists free contests)*
📖 *MovieBytes.com (film scripts and shorts)*
📖 *Science Fiction Writers of America (sfwa.org)*

#11. BOOKSTORES AND LIBRARIES

"Where is human nature so weak as in the bookstore?" – Henry Ward Beecher, 19th Century clergyman and reformer

Take advantage of your *local author* status. It makes you special. Many libraries and Independent bookstores like local authors. Walk in (so they can see you in person), show them a copy of your book, and offer some suggestions for a possible Q&A or reading, rather than a "book signing." If you have gotten your FREE Library of Congress number prior to publication, a library or bookstore may even order your book. Think in terms of what topics in your book might be of interest to the residents of that particular community. Giving a talk is also a good photo op for your website, blog, or newsletter.

A Local Box Library - Photo: Sylvia Cary

📖 *Google – search for "new bookstores"*
📖 *Indiebound.org (lists independent bookstores)*
📖 *NewShelves.com (advice on libraries)*
📖 *Publiclibraries.com (for locations)*
📖 *50states.com (facts, stats, and newspapers)*

#12. SEO WRITING

SEO means Search Engine Optimization, and SEO writing means writing articles or blog posts specifically to get picked up by Google and end up in somebody's search results when they're looking for information on your topic. That helps your book get discovered. (There's that "discoverability word again!"). A huge part of SEO writing is the strategic use of keywords to catch Google's eye. For help with keywords check out *PublisherRocket.com* (fee). People have made a science of SEO writing. Google for "How-To" info and check out SEO specialists, such as *LoriBallen.com*. She writes on real-estate, but her SEO videos work for authors doing book marketing as well.

#13. SPEAKING

If you have a good voice or have a way with words, use those as "tools" for book marketing! As the author of a published book, there are many places you can speak in addition to bookstores and libraries, both in person and on Zoom, such as writing groups, book clubs, and professional organizations and associations. Most people belong to at least one or two such groups. If your book is about teens, you can approach parenting groups, as well as mental health groups. If you write fiction, and your book takes place in another country, look up travel clubs. If the book takes place in another time period, look up history clubs, or maybe SciFi groups. Suggest yourself for an upcoming panel. Remember, you're an "expert" now. Turn your expertise into a course at a community college or adult education facility. Or an online class. Join **Toastmasters International** in your city to improve your speaking skills and practice upcoming talks. Investigate TED and TEDx talks.

Don't Forget Radio: When it comes to getting on TV as a guest, that can be difficult, especially if you're new to it, but radio is doable. There are 1000s of radio stations all over the country that gobble up 1000s of guests, and you could be one of the guests they gobble up.

Most radio gigs can be done from home. Research radio talk shows, find out how they want to be approached, and query about being interviewed.

Photo: CanvaPro

- 📖 shawguides.com (career guides & learning)
- 📖 ToastmastersInternational.org
- 📖 Ted.com (speakers on all topics)
- 📖 The Moth (live storytelling)
- 📖 Teachable.com (online classes)
- 📖 Google.com (search "speaker + topic")
- 📖 Blogtalkradio.com (opportunities to speak)

#14. NETWORKING

Photo: Canva.com

During the pandemic, in-person networking was replaced with Zoom. Zoom is a great tool, but in-person networking is its own special thing. Most writers report feeling energized and inspired when they attend a LIVE event, whether as a speaker or attendee. Enthusiasm is contagious. Ideas flow. When possible, attend events in person, such as local writing groups, conferences, or book fairs, even if it's just for a day. Check out:

📖 *meetup.com (put in your zip, search for a topic, like "writing")*
📖 *Shawguides.com (Worldwide – 6000 learning vacations and creative career programs)*
📖 *eventbrite.com (events of all kinds near you)*

#15. YOUR NEXT BOOK

"One book is never enough." – Jane Friedman

Hopefully, in this list of 15 marketing ideas, you've discovered the ones that work best for you. Maybe you've even had some fun. But inevitably there comes a time when no amount of additional marketing will help a book sell more than it has sold already. Time to move on – especially if you want a writing career. Then it's a must, because often the best way to help sell a first book is to write a second and third. At that point, you can even set up your own **book tour** by researching venues where YOUR readers hang out. Once readers pay attention to your third book, they are likely to go back and "discover" your first two books and buy them.

CLOSING QUOTE:

"I think I did pretty well considering I started out with nothing but a bunch of blank paper."
—- Actor and author Steve Martin

ABOUT THE AUTHOR

"Ever since self-publishing became a 'thing,' I've been hooked," says SYLVIA CARY, who lives in Sherman Oaks, California where she is also a licensed psychotherapist. Over the past decade, she has focused more on being a "book doctor" than being a "head doctor," and, to date, has helped some 50 other authors get published, especially self-published. She is also the author of THE THERAPIST WRITER: *Helping Mental Health Professionals Get Published.* Available on Amazon and Kindle. *SylviaCary.com* or email: *TheTherapistWriter@gmail.com.*

USEFUL PUBLISHING RESOURCES

AGENTS

- **Agentquery.com** *(database of literary agents)*
- **Duotrope.com** *(resources, agents listing)*
- **JeffHerman.com** *(proposals, agents, advice)*
- **ManuscriptWishlist.com** *(what agents want)*
- **MidwestBookReview.com** *(various resources)*
- **JaneFriedman.com** *(agent advice)*

TRADITIONAL PUBLISHING

- **Amazon.com** *(books on every aspect of publishing)*
- **Association of Christian Writers:** *ChristianWriters.co.uk*
- **Authors Guild, The**: *authorsguild.org (membership)*
- **Duotrope.com** *(resources, agents listings)*
- **Google.com** *(largest search engine)*
- **Jane Friedman's Blog**: *janefriedman.com (advice)*
- **JeffHerman.com** *(proposals, agents, advice)*
- **ManuscriptWishlist.com** *(what agents want)*
- **MidwestBookReview.com** *(all kinds of resources)*
- **Poets & Writers**: *pw.org (articles of interest)*
- **Preditors & Editors**: *pred-ed.com (warnings of scams)*
- **PublishersMarketplace.com** *(fee-based site*; *agents)*
- **QueryShark.blogspot.com** *(writing queries how-to)*
- **QueryTracker.com** *(track queries; agent database)*
- **Reedsy**: *blog.reedsy.com (articles, lists, reviews)*
- **Romance Writers of America**: *rwa.org (membership)*
- **Science Fiction and Fantasy Writers of America**: *sfwa.org*
- **SocietyofAuthors.com** *(membership org.UK)*
- **YouTube.com** *(search for tutorials on all topics)*

ACADEMIC & UNIVERSITY PUBLISHING

- **Association of University Presses, -** *aupresses.org*
- **APA Publishing**: *apa.org (American Psychological Association)*
- **Cambridge University Press**: *cambridge.org*
- **Guilford Press**: *guilford.com (an academic press)*
- **Jessica Kingsley Publishers**: *jkp.com/UK (academic press)*
- **ManuscriptWorks.com** *(academic publishing, Laura Portwood-Stacer)*
- **New Harbinger** Publications: *newharbinger.com (an cademic press)*
- **Oxford University Press**: *global.oup.com (a university press)*
- **Routledge**: *routledge.com (an academic press)*
- **Rowan & Littlefield**: *rowman.com (an academic press)*
- **SAGE Publications**: us.sagepub.com *(an academic press)*
- **University of Chicago Press:** p*ress.uchicago.edu (university)*
- **W.W. Norton & Company**: *wwnorton.com/submit-a-proposal*
- **Wiley**: *authorservices.wiley.com (an academic press)*
- **Yale University Press**: *yalebooks.yale.edu (university press)*

SELF-PUBLISHING

- **Alliance of Independent Author** - ***alli.org*** *(subscription)*
- **AprilCox.com** (*Self-Publishing Made Simple)*
- ***amarketingexpert.com*** *(Penny Sansevieri - marketing)*
- **Becca Syme** *(betterfasteracademy.com)*
- **BookStat.com** *(subscription/book industry stats)*
- **BookBub.com** *(promote self-published books, ads)*
- **Canva.com** *(graphic design; free & fee versions)*
- **Dale L. Roberts** *selfpublishingwithdale.com (Amazon expert)*
- **Dottotech.***com* *(Steve Dotto, business tech, videos, podcast)*
- **Fiverr:** *(Fiverr.com freelancers or hire)*
- **FundsforWriters.com** *(markets, streams of income – Hope Clark)*
- **ISBN** *in the US (get from bowker.com - myidentifers.com)*
- **JaneFriedman.com** *(see Resources for Writers and Blog)*
- **Joanna Penn – TheCreativePenn.com** *(podcasts/ on AI))*
- **Kindlepreneur,com** *(Dave Chesson - free courses, tools)*
- **New Shelves Books**: *newshelves.com (video tutorials)*

- **PublisherRocket.com** *(keywords, categories, competition, tools)*
- **Reedsy**: *blog.reedsy.com (all topics, freelancers for hire, advice)*
- **Science Fiction & Fantasy Writers of America** *(sfwa.org)*
- **SelfPublishingFormula.com** *(Mark Dawson)*
- **TangentTemplates.com** *(tools, templates, mockups covers)*
- **Upwork.com** *(can hire freelancers)*
- **USA Today**: *usatoday.com (has a best-seller list)*
- **Wattpad.com** *(interactive publishing)*
- **Writer Beware** blog *(sponsored by sfwa.org above)*
- **Zazzle.com** *(merch)*

ARTIFICIAL INTELIGENCE (AI)

- **Artificial Intelligence:** *Chat.openai.com (free or fee)*
- **Claude3.ai** (compared to ChatGPT 4)
- **Jane Friedman's blog:** *janefriedman.com (AI for writers)*
- **Jason West:** *info@brightlightmedia.co.uk (using AI at work)*
- **Joanna Penn** *thecreativepenn.com (podcasts on AI)*
- **Lex Fridman Podcast** *(lexfridman.com -AI topics)*
- **LifeArchitect.ai** *(lifearchitect@substack.com –"The Memo" newsletter by Dr. Alan Thompson, Australia)*
- **Matt Wolfe** *(@mreflow - YouTube weekly AI news & reviews)*
- **Midjourney.com** *(AI graphics – text-to-image)*

BOOKSTORES & LIBRARIES

- **BritishMuseum.uk** *(research)*
- **50States.com** *(facts and stats about venues)*
- **Indiebound.org** *(independent bookstores)*
- **Library of Congress** *(loc.gov)*
- **Nypl.org** *(New York Public Library-research)*
- **NewShelves.com** *(advice on getting into libraries)*
- **Newspapers.com** *(directory of newspapers worldwide)*
- **PublicLibraries.com** *(for locations of libraries)*

SPEAKING

- **Blogtalkradio.com** *(opportunities to speak on your topic)*
- **Google.com** *(search "speakers bureaus + your topic")*
- **shawguides.com** *(career guides; learning vacations)*
- **Talkersmag.com** *(about talk radio, search your topic)*
- **Teachable.com** *(create and teach online classes)*
- **Ted.com** *(speakers on all topics; Tedx.com is local)*
- **The Moth** *(live event to share storytelling)*
- **Thecreativepenn.com** podcast *(episode on audiobooks)*
- **ToastmastersInternational.org** *(speaking training)*

MISCELLANOUS

- **Book (Free download): Author Blueprint** *(revised 2024) by Joanna Penn, TheCreativePenn.com*
- **Book: The Business of Being a Writer** by Jane Friedman
- **Copyright.gov** – *to register the copyright for your book*
- **IBPA -** Ibpa_online.org) *The Independent Book Publishers Association bi-monthly magazine*
- **Low Content Publishing:** *thehomeboss.com (Nuria Corbi), paulmarles,com, Rachel Harrison-Sund.com*
- **Marketing:** *WeGrowMedia.com (Dan Blank)*
- **Music Site:** *SoundCloud.com*
- **Photo / illustrations Sites (Free)**: *creativecommons.com, Canva.com, Pixabay.com, VisualHunt.com, Unsplash.com, openclipart.org, pexels.com*

"The best way to become acquainted with a subject is to write a book about it."

– Benjamin Disraeli